MESSY AND
loved

Honest Journey,

Perfect God,

Devotional.

Copyright © 2021 by Sarah G Tomlinson
All rights reserved. No Part of this may be reproduced or copied.
Artwork & Cover by Sarah G Tomlinson.
www.littlesparrowloved.com

Your wandering in the desert is not for nothing. See it as barren, or see it as a journey where the distractions are muted, and all that is there is you and God.

— Sarah G Tomlinson

Welcome to my book Messy And Loved!

Ever wanted to read a book where you feel like you're going on a journey with someone? Ever wanted to have those... "me too" moments while reading someone else's story?

A few years ago, God prompted me to start a blog and begin writing about my thoughts. The crazy, messy, random jumble of questions, and sometimes unanswered questions, that go through my head on a daily basis.

I honestly believed I wasn't equipped enough to share my musings. I was a fiction writer, never did I think about writing my real life stuff. And I argued daily with God, about the fact I felt unqualified to share my experiences with His daughters.

But our Heavenly Father is patient, and with a little push and quite a few nudges, I finally launched Little Sparrow Loved, a blog ministry. You see, He never asked me to do anything more than share what is in my heart and finish my thoughts with His truth.

I pray as you spend time reading this book daily, weekly, over and over monthly or finish it in one giant binge, you feel as if you're journeying with me and a sisterhood is born. Because if I'm being honest, this book is about as messy as my thoughts. It is part diary, moments of testimony, a sprinkle of encouragement, a dash of scripture, short sweet prayers, and a whole lot of love for God!

Love, Sarah xx

CONTENTS

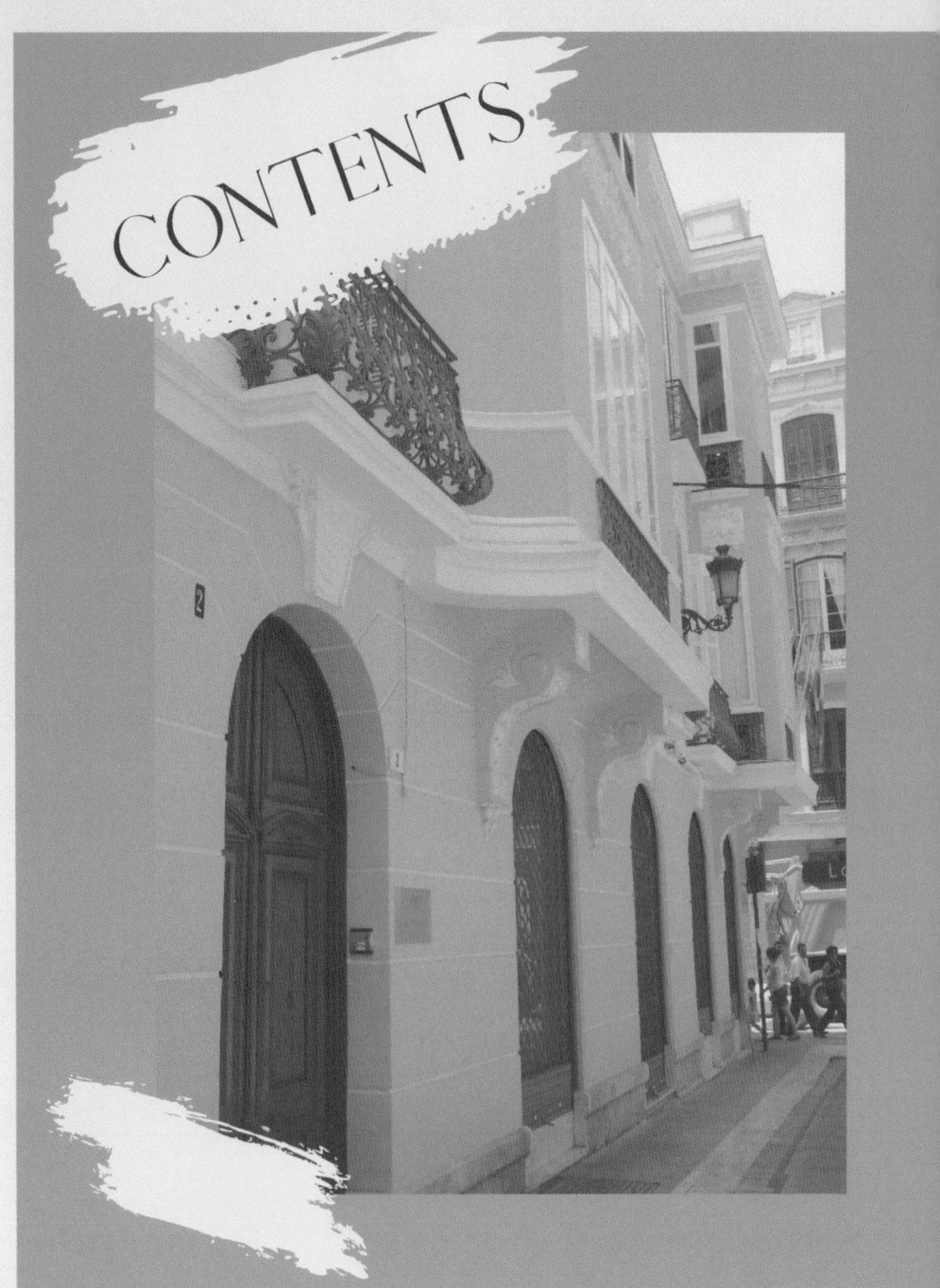

WE ALL LONG TO BE LOVED
HAS ANYBODY TOLD YOU?
YOU ARE BRAVE
BUT GOD DOES
WHOLE LOT OF BRAVE
BE YOUR UNIQUE SELF
MINISTRY STARTS WITH YOU
SHE IS BEAUTIFUL
I'M JUST A NOBODY
STOP FOR A MOMENT
GOD WANTS YOUR MESSY
IT'S THE CONVERSATIONS
YOU HAVE PAIN?
ALL FIGURED OUT
I'M SENSITIVE
MESSY GRACE
I'M NOT AFRAID
SHE IS A WARRIOR
GRIEF
LIFE IS MESSY

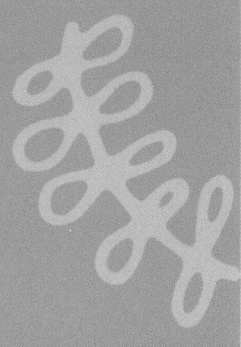

we all long to be loved...

We all long to be loved. We all seek to have a connection and be understood, to be valued and have our worth seen.

Many times in my life, I believed that once I got married I would find all that, then when I had children who would offer me unconditional love, I would definitely feel all that. The biggest shock came after those beautiful things happened in my life, but I still didn't feel whole. I still craved this unwavering wholeness that never came.

I remember watching my children ride their bikes one day and as I smiled at their efforts, I whispered to the Lord, "I am so blessed, so why do I still feel like it's not enough? That I am not enough?"

That's when the Lord began to show me that the love I seek in others will never be enough, because my heart longs for His kind of love. My worth will never come from others acceptance, it's about truly understanding my worth in God's eyes and not the opinion of others. It's getting to a place where all we seek is those moments with God where He will fill us with that unshakable knowing that we are more than enough! That we are precious, listened to, and most of all treasured beyond measure. That is when we begin to feel the love we so desperately seek. When we seek Love itself.

Love, Sarah xx

VERSE

And so we know and rely on the love God has for us. God is love. Whoever lives in love lives in God, and God in them. - 1 John 4:16

PRAYER

Lord,

Thank you that I can come to you and find the love I so desperately seek. Help me to see more of you and what is held within your hands for me, like a love I will never know from anyone else. Let me see always that I am enough and all I need comes from you.

In Jesus' name, Amen.

WRITE YOUR THOUGHTS HERE

....
....
....
....
....
....
....

Has Anybody Told You?

Has anybody told you how amazing you are today?
How treasured and loved you are? Well... they are about to!

I am going to tell you all the things I know God longs to whisper into your heart daily because He adores you beyond your wildest imagination! So now is the time to listen.

You are loved.
You are treasured.
You are being cheered on.
You are held when it hurts.
You are always smiled upon.
You are never alone.
You are uniquely made.
You are one of a kind.
You are a brilliant work in progress.
You are beautiful.
You are strong.
You are courageous, and that's just a small list of all that you are.

Most of all... you are a daughter of the Most High King!

Love, Sarah xx

VERSE

I praise you because I am fearfully and wonderfully made; your works are wonderful, I know that full well.
- Psalm 139:14

PRAYER

Lord,

May I stand on your truth today, that I am loved and seen by you. Help me to focus on your word and my very purpose for being born. You do not make mistakes and I am exactly who you called me to be. May I stand on your promises and also help others to see how amazing they are in your eyes.

In Jesus' name, Amen.

WRITE YOUR THOUGHTS HERE

....
....
....
....
....
....
....

Brave... it's such a powerful word that means ready to endure danger or pain, to show courage, to find strength. So often we want to hide beneath the covers and hope that somehow trials will pass us by. That the hurt and rejection will magically disappear and the struggles we face no longer seem so big.

But what happens when we find our Brave? When we stand up and take on every giant that blocks our way?

We find our strength, we gain wisdom, we realise that God has been with us the entire way, preparing us for this moment! We acquire a new testimony, we encourage others, and we are now prepared to take on the next mountain because we know we can! Because we are conquerors, warriors, daughters of the Most High! With power from speaking just one name... Jesus!

So, I want you to find your Brave today. It may look different from someone else's, and that's okay. You may jump out of the gates with fire in your heart, or you may take slow steady steps forward. However you stand, that's okay! Because God is there to lead you, stand beside you and fight for you the entire way, Brave beautiful girl.

Love, Sarah xx

BUT WHAT HAPPENS WHEN WE FIND OUR BRAVE? WHEN WE STAND UP AND TAKE ON EVERY GIANT THAT BLOCKS OUR WAY?

-SARAH TOMLINSON

VERSE

"Be strong and courageous. Do not be afraid or terrified because of them, for the Lord your God goes with you; he will never leave you nor forsake you." - Deuteronomy 31:6

PRAYER

Lord,
Help me stand strong and brave today. Remind me always that remaining in your word and placing on your armour daily is what will give me strength. Not only for myself, but that I can always stand for those around me also.

In Jesus' name, Amen.

WRITE YOUR THOUGHTS HERE

....
....
....
....
....
....
....
....

But God Does

I don't know the pain you may feeling, but God does.

I don't know the hurt you may be carrying, but God does.

I don't know the battle you may be in the middle of, but God does.

I don't know the mountain you may be climbing, but God does.

Beautiful daughters, don't let the weight of other peoples' judgment weigh you down. Let the weight of God's love rest on your shoulders instead.

Don't let your circumstances dictate your status or standing. Let God's truth be at the forefront of you thoughts.

Because you, my darling, are a daughter of a King. Loved. Cherished. Created with purpose. And you are strong and can withstand anything that tries to hold you down.

That is your superpower.

Love, Sarah xx

Where I am

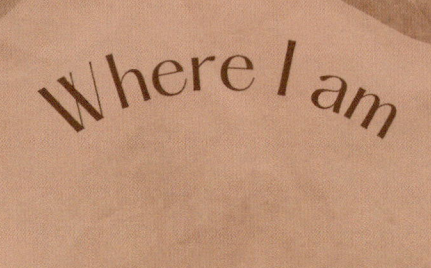

MESSY

He is orderly.

VERSE

She gave this name to the Lord who spoke to her: "You are the God who sees me," for she said, "I have now seen the One who sees me.- Genesis 16:13

PRAYER

Lord,
May your eyes always gaze upon me. Let my heart rest in the knowledge that you see me even when others don't. May I always remember that you are in every aspect of my life and that you call me by name.

In Jesus' name, Amen.

WRITE YOUR THOUGHTS HERE

....
....
....
....
....
....

Whole Lot of Grace

I don't always have the answers. Truth is most days I feel like I know nothing much at all.

But in that there's a vulnerability I'm sharing with you all. I'm showing a chink in my armour and saying that it's okay to not always be indestructible. I make mistakes, I sometimes feel too deep and that clouds my logic. I'm saying that not having all the answers stops me from lecturing others on their decisions also.

But what I do have is empathy, open arms, a heart that will love, a mouth streaming prayers for those that need it, and a truth in my spirit that I know a God that does have the answers.

I think that makes me brave. Brave enough to give myself permission to not be right all the time. Brave enough to realise I still have a lot to learn. Brave enough to come alongside my fellow sisters and remind them that it's okay to not always have the answers either.

Because one thing we do have is a whole lot of grace.

Love, Sarah xx

One thing we do have is a whole lot of grace.

VERSE

Out of his fullness we have all received grace in place of grace already given. - John 1:16

PRAYER

Lord,
Keep my heart pliable and soft today. I know I may not have all the answers. I know I am not immune from the hurts of the world around, but, Father, I have you. A God that sees my hurt, sees my heart, and gives me grace daily. Please help me to be more like you and show that same grace to others.

In Jesus' name, Amen.

WRITE YOUR THOUGHTS HERE

....
....
....
....
....
....

Growing up, I used to think I had to be the perfect church girl. Dress nice, have a humbleness about me, and play the part of someone who had it all together because Christ was so woven into her fabric that she was... well, perfect.

Even as life was throwing volcano-sized rocks at me, I still held onto that image that somewhere, someday, I was going to resemble that woman I had built up in my mind. Fast forward 30 years later and I am still not that woman. No, instead I'm the woman who ties her hair into a messy bun 95 percent of my days. I'm the woman who thinks that leggings are the greatest piece of clothing to ever grace her closet. I'm the woman who sings worship at the top of her lungs on every car ride. I'm the woman who loses her patience with her kids more than she likes to admit. I'm the woman who's always 15 minutes late to everything no matter how hard she tries to rush everyone into the car. And... I'm the woman who brings dessert bought from a shop on the way to an event, knowing her cooking will set the smoke alarm off before it leaves her oven.

And I'm happy being her. I'm happy knowing that God broke the mould when he made me. I'm happy that a pastor once told me I was a rebellious Christian. Because Jesus, too, went against the grain for what He stood for.

So beautiful daughters of God, throw away the idea that one day you're going to be the perfect image of an altogether Christian woman and break the rules! Be messy, be fallible, be unique, and become the perfect image of Christ. BE YOU! The you God created you to be. Because you never know who needs to see that it doesn't always have to be perfect in order to follow Jesus.

Be blessed. Be a light.
Love, Sarah xx

Beautiful daughters of God, throw away the idea that one day you're going to be the perfect image of an altogether Christian woman and break the rules!

SARAH TOMLINSON

VERSE

"So God created mankind in his own image, in the image of God he created them; male and female he created them." – Genesis 1:27 NIV

PRAYER

Lord,

Thank you for pursuing me, even when I can't see my own worth. You remind me daily that I am loved, treasured, and adored. It's right there in your truthful word. Help me to love myself more and recognise that I was fearfully and wonderfully made, because you knew me in the womb.

In Jesus' name, Amen.

WRITE YOUR THOUGHTS HERE

....
....
....
....
....
....
....
....

Ministry Starts With You

Ministry starts with you. Right where you are, with the people that surround you every day. The ones that you know and the strangers who will be sent your way.

Sharing the love of God was never meant to be confined to four walls. What happens within the walls are equipping you to step out into the open world and witness, support, shine the light, and salt the earth with the Holy word and the Father's heart.

We only need to look at the life of Jesus to see He was everywhere the people could reach Him. He was in the places our arms need to extend and our feet follow in His footsteps.

So beautiful daughters, don't settle yourself with what feels safe. Step out from the four walls with the knowledge that God has big plans and an intentional purpose for your life. Dare to go, be brave enough to reach out and minister to the people in the places that Jesus needs you to be.

Love, Sarah xx

We only need to look at the life of Jesus to see He was everywhere the people could reach Him.

-SARAH TOMLINSON

VERSE

"Come, follow me," Jesus said, "and I will send you out to fish for people." - Matthew 4:19 NIV

PRAYER

Lord,

Give me the courage to reach out and be a light for you in their lives. Help me to live authentically and share your love in my every day walk with those I know and the strangers I will meet along the way. Let my voice be your mouthpiece and the wisdom that passes my lips to come from the Holy Spirit.

In Jesus' name, Amen.

WRITE YOUR THOUGHTS HERE

....
....
....
....
....
....
....

She is beautiful that girl you see in the mirror.
You study her close, picking out every flaw, every spot, wrinkle, or imperfection. You probably wished you had curly hair or straight. You long to be taller or shorter, curvier or thinner. You see the small lines that must have come up over night or the new grey that appeared in a blink. All of it staring you in the face as you gaze at your reflection.

But no matter what you're thinking or criticising, that girl you see in the mirror is beautiful.

So look a little closer, truly look at the woman who was once a girl, a youth, a young lady... and admire her. Haven't you noticed yet? Those eyes are shining and reflecting a perfect person, created in the image of God! No mistake made, no fault to be found. Just a uniqueness that only you have, a smile like no other, a laugh so distinct. She radiates sunshine to the darkness around her. She glows with a light that was gifted to her before she was even born.

Imago dei... she whispers to herself until she believes it.

Imago dei... Image of God. Because that is what she carries. That is her likeness, her identity, her birthright.

She is beautiful that girl you see in the mirror.

Love, Sarah xx

She radiates sunshine to the darkness around her. She glows with a light that was gifted to her before she was even born.

-SARAH TOMLINSON

VERSE

And we all, with unveiled face, beholding the glory of the Lord, are being transformed into the same image from one degree of glory to another. For this comes from the Lord who is the Spirit. - 2 Corinthians 3:18

PRAYER

Lord,
Thank you for molding me in your image and yet making me so unique that there is no one else like me. Help me to see the beauty in myself and to always remember that you created me to be exactly who I was meant to be. May I show my gratitude to you daily and help others to see themselves the way you see them also.

In Jesus' name, Amen.

WRITE YOUR THOUGHTS HERE

....
....
....
....
....
....

I'm Just a Nobody

"I'm nobody. How can God use me?"

That is something I hear from the mouths of many daughters of God more often than I can count, and it breaks my heart.

But being me, I always look back at them and assure them with the truth. "Jesus loves the nobody, the struggling, the sick, and the poor. How can we share that truth with those that need it if we don't believe it ourselves?"

Beautiful daughters, let me tell you today that the nobody is a somebody to Christ, and that somebody needs to see and hear the love of God from a person who knows that their identity and worth was paid for at the cross.

You were born with purpose, with a call, with a task, and being a nobody is not a part of God's plan for your life.

Love, Sarah xx

You are a somebody!

You were born with purpose, with a call, with a task, and being a nobody is not a part of God's plan for your life.

VERSE

But you are a chosen people, a royal priesthood, a holy nation, God's special possession, that you may declare the praises of Him who called you out of darkness into His wonderful light. - 1 Peter 2:9

PRAYER

Lord,
Thank you for your amazing and unending love. Help me to remember to repeat these words to myself daily until they root themselves in my spirit. I am loved, I am treasured, I am called, and I am a very wanted somebody. In Jesus' name, Amen.

WRITE YOUR THOUGHTS HERE

....
....
....
....
....
....
....
....

Stop for a Moment

Let's just stop a moment.
Take a deep breath.
Close your eyes.
Focus on Jesus.
And whisper the word… "Peace."

Try not to worry for just the briefest of time as to what tomorrow holds. Try not to think of the pain of yesterday for the smallest of seconds and just focus on the now.

Life is a story that has and will unfold. There's no getting around it as the pages continue to fill up and turn. The tests of the yesterdays become the testimonies of the future. So sit a little while in the page of today. Be thankful, be pliant, be open and ready. But most of all, thank Him for every paragraph of your life He continues to help you pen and rest in the peace.

Love, Sarah xx

Try not to worry for just the briefest of time as to what tomorrow holds.

VERSE

"Therefore I tell you, do not worry about your life, what you will eat or drink; or about your body, what you will wear. Is not life more than food, and the body more than clothes?" -Matthew 6:25

PRAYER

Lord,
Help me to keep my eyes and thoughts on the things I can do today. Let me give the future over to you with trust from my very being, and to hand the wounds of my past gratefully into your forgiving hands.

In Jesus' name, Amen.

WRITE YOUR THOUGHTS HERE

....
....
....
....
....
....
....
....

God Wants Your Messy

God wants your messy.
Every single piece of your messy. Not perfection, not a facade, not a picture perfect representation of a got-it-all-together life.

No, he wants the broken pieces, the addictions, the grief, the confusion, the loss, the pain, and everything else that plagues you.

Better yet, He wants you to take that messy and use it. Bare it to all that walk your way, for in that messiness is where His light will shine through. People will wonder, without saying a word, "What makes her so strong?" And in that you can reply, "A saviour that carries my burdens and loves me right where I am. And if you're brave enough to come alongside me, we can do messy together."

Love, Sarah xx

For in that messiness is where His light will shine through.

VERSE

Praise be to the God and Father of our Lord Jesus Christ, the Father of compassion and the God of all comfort, for who comforts us in all our troubles, so that we can comfort those in any trouble with the comfort we ourselves receive from God. -2 Corinthians 1:3-4

PRAYER

Lord,
I pray today that I see the lessons in my messy moments. I thank you that you love me and hold me up with your righteous hands as I walk through each season. Guide me to be authentic in all aspects of my life and to let others know they can come to you no matter what they face.

In Jesus' name, Amen.

WRITE YOUR THOUGHTS HERE

....
....
....
....
....
....
....

It's the Conversations

It's the conversations that happen behind the scenes that mean the most.

Those are the words that stuck out to me with truth at the recent women's conference I attended.

As great as it is to hear the words of encouragement at speaking engagements or read uplifting blog posts, it's the unedited, gritty, raw conversations behind the scenes that mean the most.

I have to get real with you all when I tell you there is nothing more refreshing and soothing to my soul as when I hear from another woman about her imperfections and failings. When the honesty about parenting, women's problems, marriage, self-worth, and faith shortcomings are spoken about openly, I listen and I go... me too!

All of a sudden I'm no longer feeling alone or like a failure because I have met someone living out their God-given life with problems just like me. Even if they've walked through them and come out the other side, they remind me that they've been there and all is going to be okay.

So to all the beautiful ladies out there unafraid to share their stories and trials... you are my people! Keep being brave, keep speaking bold, keep encouraging others. Through your truthful, raw, honesty, others will rise up and speak their truth, too, bare their struggles and imperfections, and encourage someone else.

Be blessed. Be a light.
Love, Sarah xx

all the feels

So to all the beautiful ladies out there unafraid to share their stories and trials... you are my people! Keep being brave, keep speaking bold, keep encouraging others.

VERSE

And let us consider how we may spur one another on toward love and good deeds, not giving up meeting together, as some are in the habit of doing, but encouraging one another—and all the more as you see the Day approaching. -Hebrews 10:24-25

PRAYER

Lord,
Guide me in how to show others grace, acceptance, and love. Help me to open up and talk about the real things in my life with honesty and show others that I, in turn, am there for them also.

In Jesus' name, Amen.

WRITE YOUR THOUGHTS HERE

....
....
....
....
....
....
....

You Have Pain?

You have pain?
I will be your balm.

You have hurt?
I will carry the load.

Feeling broken?
I will glue your pieces.

Struggling with emotions?
I will guide you with truth.

Not sure of your path?
I will direct the way.

Want to know your purpose?
I have given you dreams.

Don't you see that no matter what,
I will always be with you.

I want you to remember this always—
Life is going to be messy, never
perfect, never easy.
It wasn't supposed to be.

But I see you,
I see all that you do,
And you are loved.

Love, God xx

Life is going to be messy, never perfect, never easy.
It wasn't supposed to be.

VERSE

Record my misery; list my tears on your scroll —
are they not in your record? Then my enemies will turn
back when I call for help. By this I will know that God is
for me. In God, whose word I praise, in the Lord, whose
word I praise—in God I trust and am not afraid.
What can man do to me? -Hebrews 10:24-25

PRAYER

Lord,
What more can I say today except thank you. You are a
good, good Father that always brings me comfort,
collects my tears, and promises that I am made new each
day. I will sing you praises with every breath that leaves
my lungs.

In Jesus' name, Amen.

WRITE YOUR THOUGHTS HERE

....
....
....
....
....
....
....

All Figured Out

People often think that because we attach the word Christian to our identity that we have it all figured out.

And in truth, they are right.

We figured out that life can still be hard.
We figured out that we still have to slay our giants.
We figured out that there are mountains we still have to climb.
We figured out that we stumble often.
We figured out that grief, heartache, and illness still penetrate our armour.
We figured out that we need to find joy in the chaos.
We figured out that faith outweighs fear.
We figured out we need grace daily.
We figured out we cannot do life on our own.
We figured out that we need a saviour.
We figured out that we were born for a purpose.
Most of all, we figured out that we are loved by Love itself—the creator, the Father, the great I AM!

So yeah, we do have it all figured out.

Love, Sarah xx

We are loved by Love itself.

VERSE

Jesus looked at them and said, "With man this is impossible, but with God all things are possible." –Matthew 19:26

PRAYER

Lord,
I know that with you all things are possible. May I always read your word and soak your truth into my spirit. May you impart wisdom to me and teach me to always rely on your strength and remember that with you, I can achieve so much. Because I figured out that you are the great I Am and I need you every day for eternity.

In Jesus' name, Amen.

WRITE YOUR THOUGHTS HERE

....
....
....
....
....
....
....
....

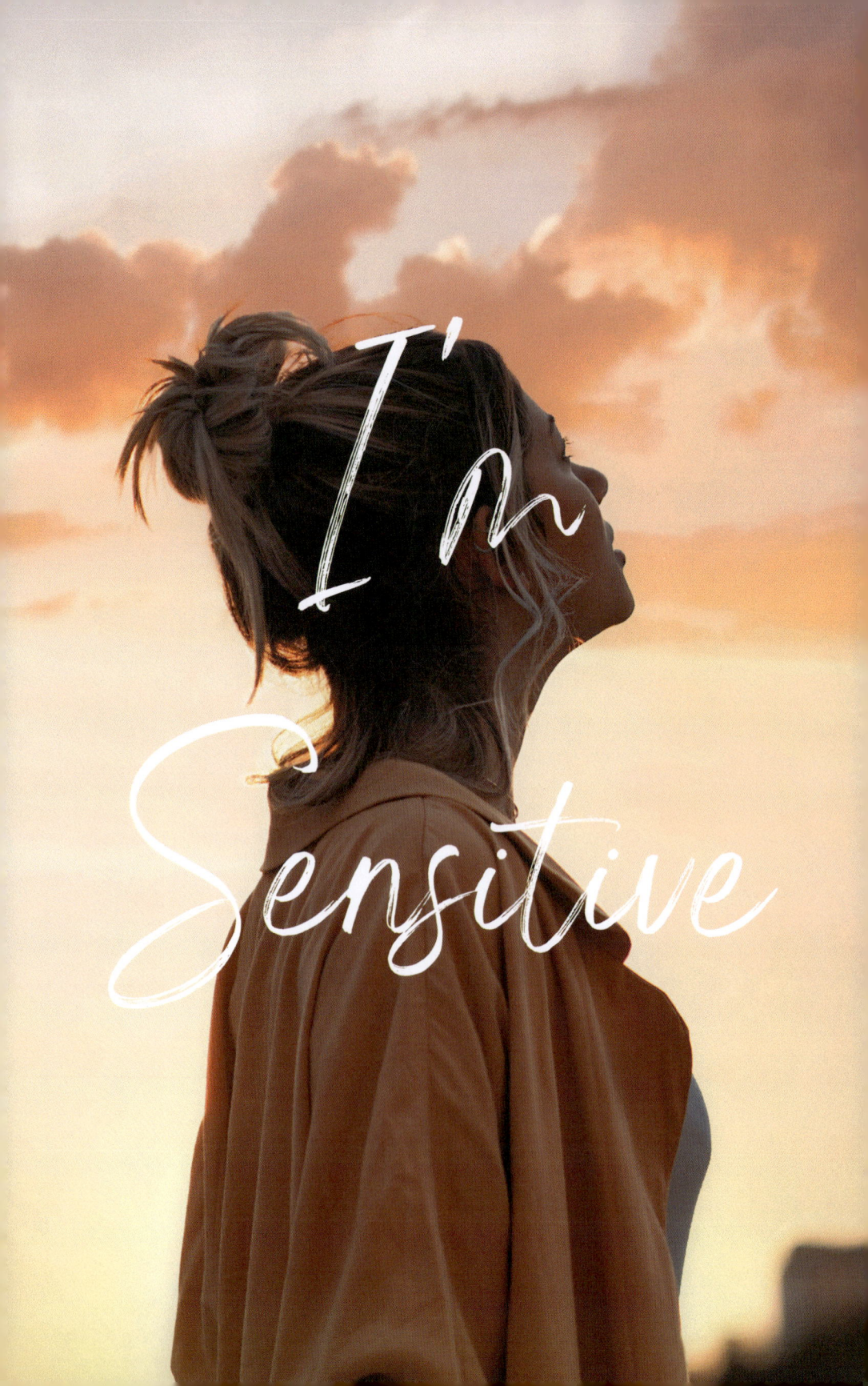

I'm Sensitive

I'm a sensitive person.
I'm sensitive to comments, I'm sensitive to the feelings of others and I'm sensitive to the pain that this world is going through. So much so, my prayers are long with petitions and my nights are even longer as I lay awake thinking of all the things that need fixing.

I used to think that this feeling was a weakness, as my heart hurt over the smallest things and the crushing weight of knowing that me... just one little person couldn't save those that needed it the most. Knowing I couldn't take away the sadness, the tears, the grief or regrets of those around me, crushed my soul.

But then I realised that being sensitive is a mighty gift from above. It pairs with empathy, mercy, understanding, a soft shoulder and a patient ear. And the lyrics by Casting Crowns slips into my mind over and over, "Father, break our hearts for what breaks yours."

I learned that those sensitive to the hearts of man and the whisperings of the Spirit are some of the greatest intercessors and prayer warriors.

And then I don't feel alone, I don't feel like one little me is no longer enough. Because out there are others like me! Brothers and sisters in Christ, feeling so deep it's almost suffocating.

They are faithfully trusting in a God who is sufficient and meets our needs; they are praying and their prayers come alongside mine for the people in their lives, their church, their cities, their nations, the hungry, the abused, and the broken. With a war cry, we are praying for those that we will never even meet.

And no matter how many times I am put down, hurt, betrayed, or dismissed, I will still forgive, love, and ask God to bless those I have had the opportunity to meet and those I may never meet. I pray that He will guide them, fight for them, rescue them, be their safe place, and let them see His love. Because I am sensitive and what a gift that is to have.

Love, Sarah xx

VERSE

Be kind and compassionate to one another, forgiving each other, just as in Christ God forgave you.
-Ephesians 4:32

PRAYER

Lord,
Thank you for giving me a soft and tender heart of mercy. Keep it from bitterness as I share my love with those around me and understand their plight. Help me to embrace who I am and accept that my sensitivity is a blessing and gift from you for purposes you have waiting for me.

In Jesus' name, Amen.

WRITE YOUR THOUGHTS HERE

....
....
....
....
....
....
....

Messy Grace

Messy Grace

I don't always have the answers.
I have asked time and time again, "God, why?"
I've struggled with forgiveness, my messy thoughts running wild.

Moments have been tough, a new mountain a new day. I've climbed it to the peak only to see another hurdle barreling my way.

I lower my head, tears rolling down my face.
"I don't think I can do it, Lord. I cannot run this race. I'm all kinds of messy, my thoughts, my life, my pain. Can't you take this burden and clear the path I pray?"

Then I hear the whisper, and feel the gentle touch as God whispers in my ear. "Sweet One, you can do this, for I have made you tough. I am always with you, arms open to hold you close. Come to me with your messy for you are mine just as I had hoped."

And in that quiet moment as I looked into the vastness of the valleys, I felt the grace of my Father covering all my messy.

So I follow in His footsteps and offer others the same grace.

You are loved here, no conditions, and I'll walk the mountainside with you. Your messy is wanted here, because Christ wants you, too.

Written by Sarah Tomlinson

So I follow in His footsteps and offer others the same grace.

VERSE

But he said to me, "My grace is sufficient for you, for my power is made perfect in weakness." Therefore I will boast all the more gladly of my weaknesses, so that the power of Christ may rest upon me. -2 Corinthians 12:9

PRAYER

Lord,
I may not have all the answers or the strength at times, but I will sing of your praises daily. My strength comes from you. My sins forgiven because of you. My grace will be offered to others because you offer me the same grace daily.

In Jesus' name, Amen.

WRITE YOUR THOUGHTS HERE

....
....
....
....
....
....
....

I Am Not Afraid

I'm not afraid to say that I live a roller coaster life of emotions.

I'm not afraid to say that I don't always get things right.

I'm not afraid to say that I struggle to forgive at times.

I'm not afraid to say that I am beautiful.

I'm not afraid to say that am loved beyond measure.

I'm not afraid to say that I am given grace daily.

I'm not afraid to say I love Jesus.

I'm not afraid to say that I am a woman of God.

I am not afraid... No, I am brave!

Love, Sarah xx

I AM NOT AFRAID... NO, I AM BRAVE!

VERSE

The Lord himself goes before you and will be with you; he will never leave you nor forsake you. Do not be afraid; do not be discouraged." -Deuteronomy 3:8

PRAYER

Lord,
Today I pray for strength and courage. Your word says that I need not be afraid for you are with me always. Give me the courage to do what you need me to do, for I can do nothing without your support and guidance.

In Jesus' name, Amen.

WRITE YOUR THOUGHTS HERE

....
....
....
....
....
....
....
....

She is a Warrior

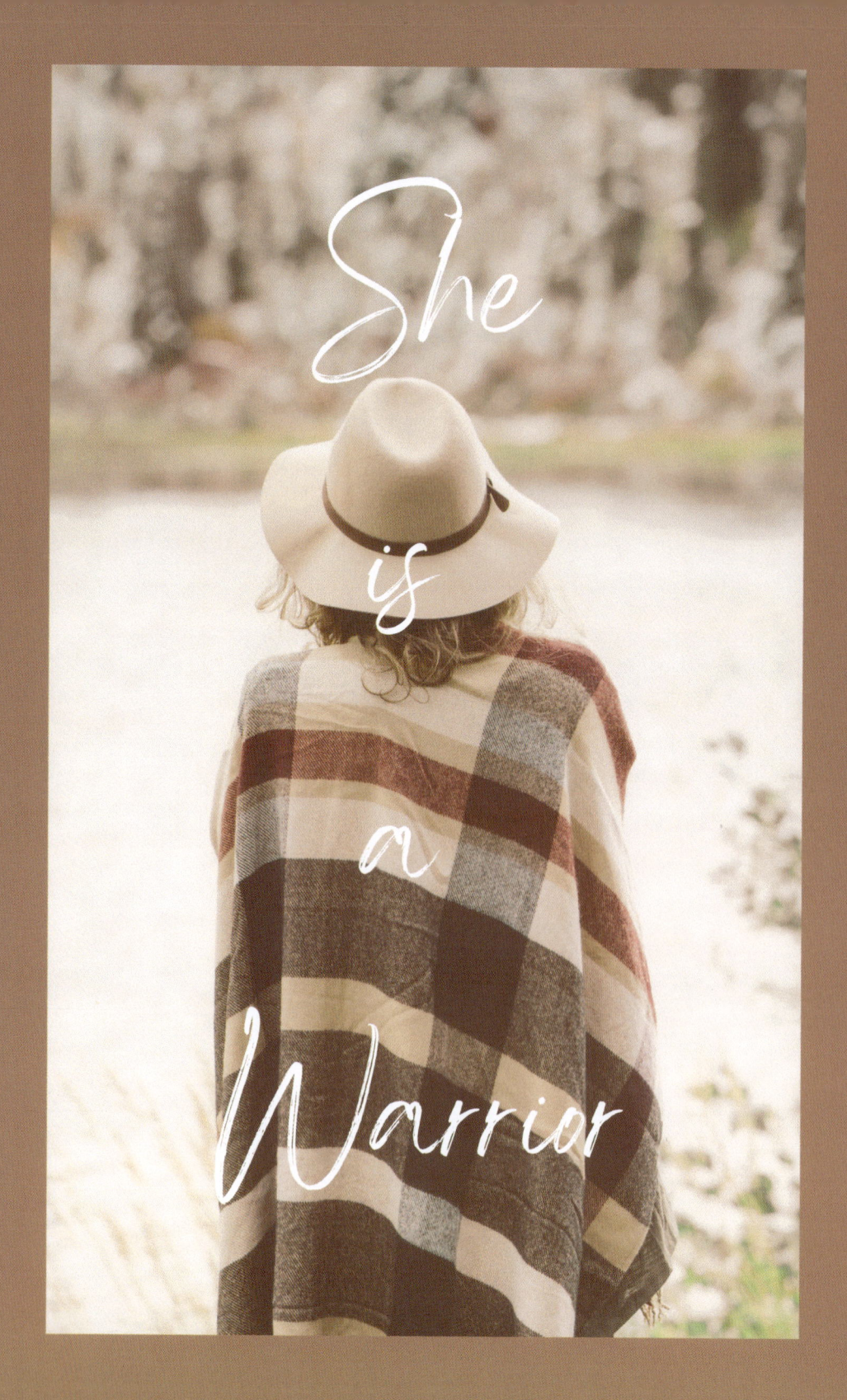

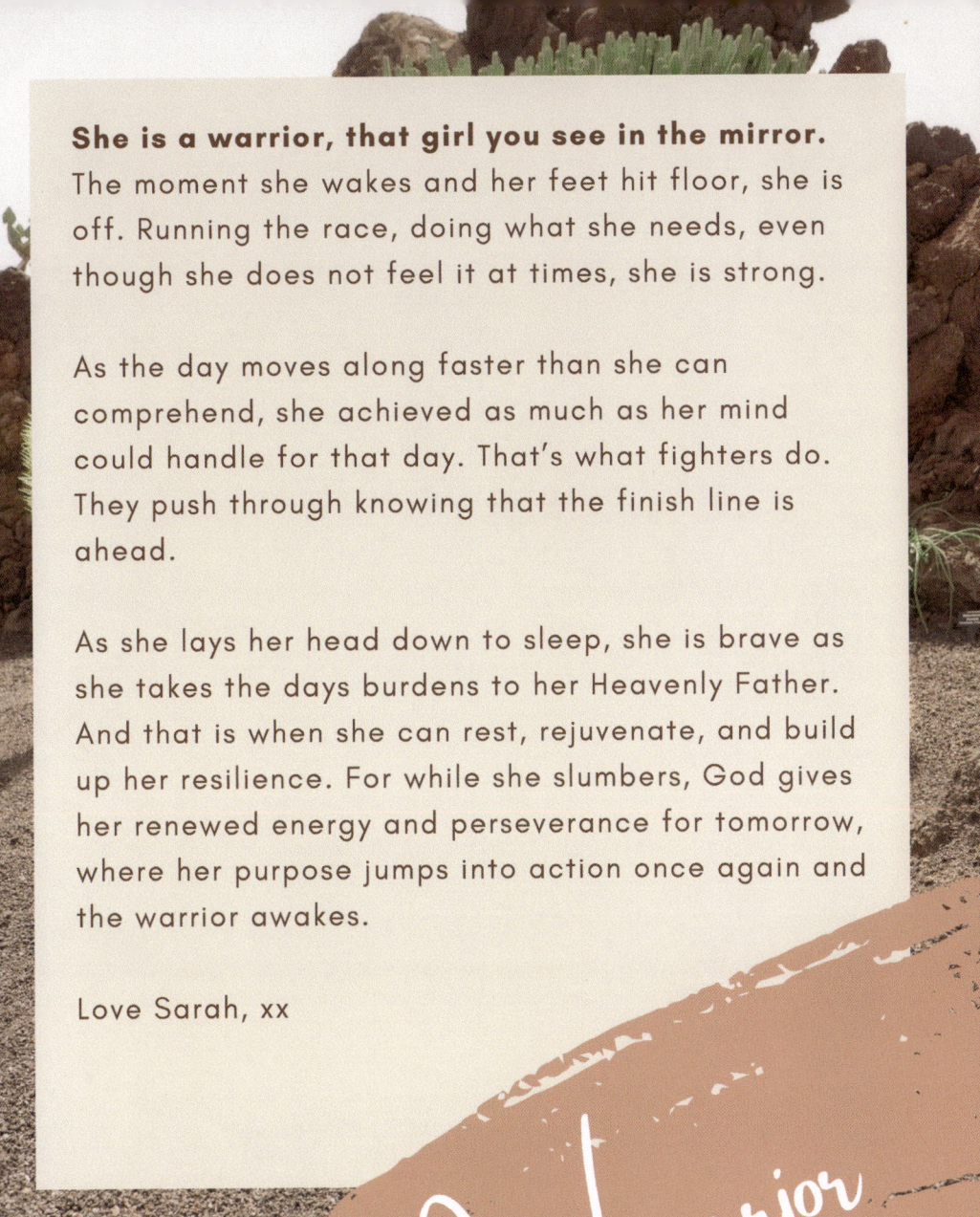

She is a warrior, that girl you see in the mirror. The moment she wakes and her feet hit floor, she is off. Running the race, doing what she needs, even though she does not feel it at times, she is strong.

As the day moves along faster than she can comprehend, she achieved as much as her mind could handle for that day. That's what fighters do. They push through knowing that the finish line is ahead.

As she lays her head down to sleep, she is brave as she takes the days burdens to her Heavenly Father. And that is when she can rest, rejuvenate, and build up her resilience. For while she slumbers, God gives her renewed energy and perseverance for tomorrow, where her purpose jumps into action once again and the warrior awakes.

Love Sarah, xx

Warrior

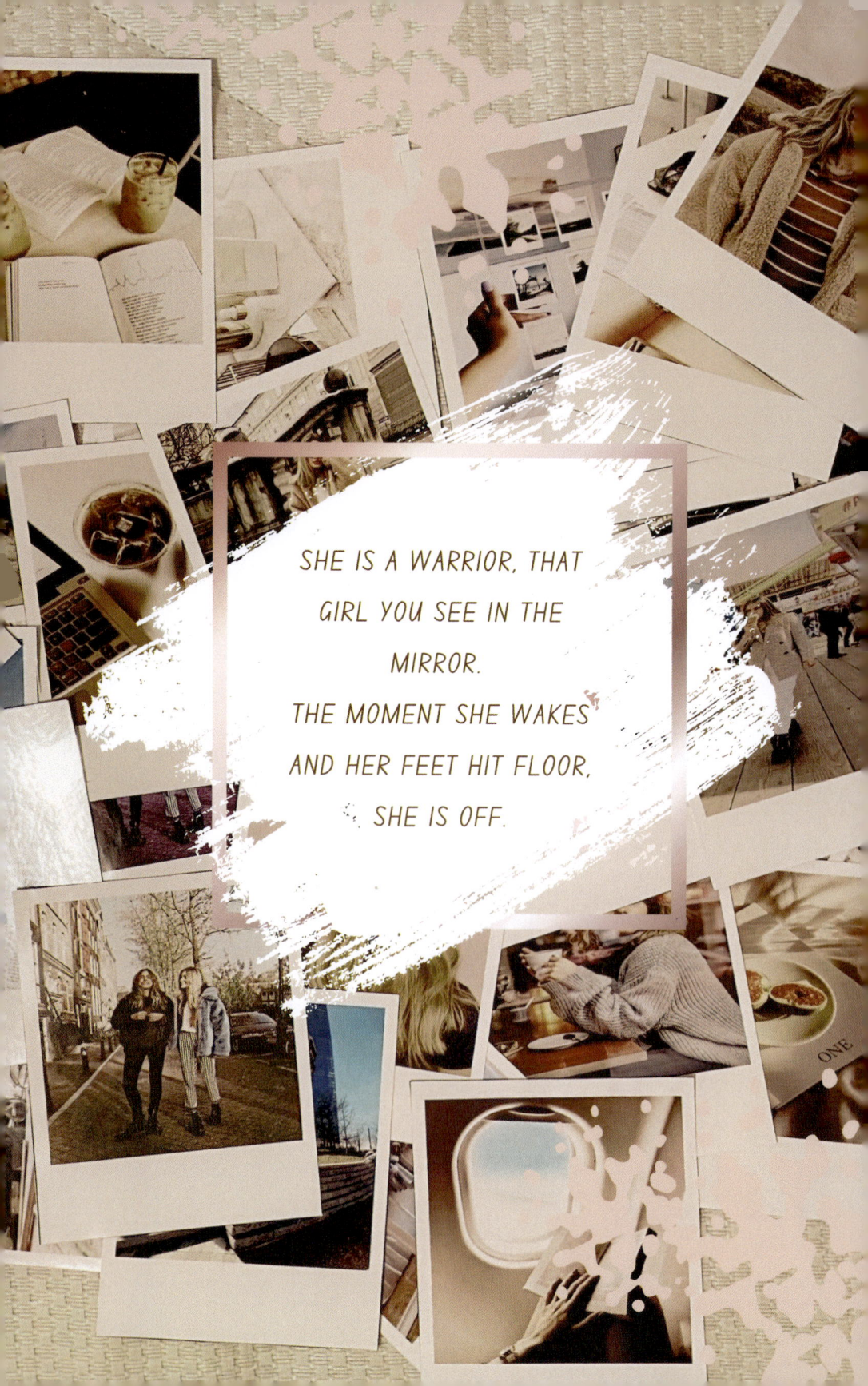

SHE IS A WARRIOR, THAT
GIRL YOU SEE IN THE
MIRROR.
THE MOMENT SHE WAKES
AND HER FEET HIT FLOOR,
SHE IS OFF.

VERSE

She is clothed with strength and dignity; she can laugh at the days to come. She speaks with wisdom, and faithful instruction is on her tongue. She watches over the affairs of her household and does not eat the bread of idleness.
-Proverbs 31:25-27

PRAYER

Lord,
Help me to endure the call you have placed on my life with joy in my heart. May I rise each morning with renewed strength and drown out the enemy's voice that comes to discourage me. Clothe me with grace and protect my health, strength, joy, and humbleness.

In Jesus' name, Amen.

WRITE YOUR THOUGHTS HERE

....
....
....
....
....
....
....

Grief...

Grief... It's something that affects every single one of us. There's no getting around the feeling of complete loss, the emptiness that emotion holds, the pain that rips at your chest until you can't breathe.

We cannot even put a time limit on how long grief can last. It could be hours, days, years, or the rest of your life. It's not reserved just for lost loved ones; it's the separation of a child, it's the empty womb you are longing to be filled, the broken marriage, the lost friendship, the illness that ravages the bodies of those we treasure.

Like I said, grief comes in all forms and there is no escape. But there is an answer, even when you struggle to hear it.

I felt God saying to me tonight, "It's okay to be angry and sad. Just be sure you don't stay there. I may not give you the answers you want, but I will answer in a way I will one day reveal to you. So be angry, but when you're ready, I am waiting, right beside you, because I love you more than you could ever feel or understand."

I don't know what you may be going through, but I bet you know someone who could use comfort today. The best way to show them we see them, hear them and love them is to open up our home to them. Speak face to face, share a coffee and really listen. Then when you are alone, pray for them, pray for yourself, and seek the Lord, even in the grief, because joy will be found in Him again. Even if it's not today.

Love, Sarah xx

I DON'T KNOW WHAT YOU MAY BE GOING THROUGH, BUT I BET YOU KNOW SOMEONE WHO COULD USE COMFORT TODAY.

VERSE

The LORD is close to the brokenhearted and saves those who are crushed in spirit. -Psalm 34:18

PRAYER

Lord,
Grant me joy even as I walk through this grief with pain and hurt filling my heart. Envelope me with peace and assurance as I wade through this heavy time in my life. Help me to see the sun again as it peeks out from behind the grey clouds with the promise of a brighter day to come.

In Jesus' name, Amen.

WRITE YOUR THOUGHTS HERE

....
....
....
....
....
....
....

Life is Messy

To the woman reading this,

Life is messy. No matter how hard we try to pin down the routine, promise ourselves that tomorrow we will make the effort to get out of our leggings and put on some makeup, not yell at the kids, ring someone we should have weeks ago, finish a task or bake from scratch.

No matter what we do, something happens and we fall short of the expectation we placed on ourselves.

There are going to be numerous times a day we let ourselves, our children, maybe our job or friends down. How do I know that? Because we are not perfect. And we will never get close to being perfect. Because like I said above, life is messy.

From the junk drawer we don't want people to see, to the food containers in the car, to the mountain of laundry, to the emotions we battle through daily, the relationships that take so much effort, to the figuring out of our purpose—it is all one messy roller coaster of a ride that we need to hang on to and along the way, throw our hands up and embrace it.

You don't see it now, but you will when you look back one day. The growth, the wisdom, the lessons are all a part of the checklist. You've changed without even knowing it. Learning to let go of the things that drain you and embracing the things that strengthen.

So yeah, life feels messy, but your story isn't finished yet.

Love, Sarah xx

VERSE

"For I know the plans I have for you," declares the LORD, "plans to prosper you and not to harm you, plans to give you hope and a future." -Jeremiah 29:11

PRAYER

Lord,

I praise You that You have given me life and made me a new creation in Christ. Thank You, Father, for You have a purpose for my life. Help me to fulfil all that You would have me do and may I be obedient to Your voice.

In Jesus' name, Amen.

WRITE YOUR THOUGHTS HERE

....
....
....
....
....
....
....

ABOUT THE AUTHOR

Be Blessed

Sarah G Tomlinson is a wife, mother, author, and creator. When she's not running around after her family, you will find her typing away and encouraging others on her website and Christian online ministry Little Sparrow Loved.

When she isn't doing that, you will also find her lost in make believe worlds as she works on her inspirational romance, devotionals, speculative fantasy fiction, or creating products for her Etsy Shop.

She loves being a daughter of God, embraces her messy, shares her thoughts openly, and counts her blessings.

If she's not doing any of the above, you will find her reading in a quiet corner, hoping for rain so she can stay inside all day and snuggle up under her blankets, sporting a messy bun, leggings and an oversized jumper.

She loves to hear from her readers and spends way too much time on her Little Sparrow Loved Facebook page.

You can follow her here-

www.littlesparrowloved.com
facebook.com/littlesparrowloved
Facebook.com/authorsarahgtomlinson
instagran.com/littlesparrowloved
instagram.com/authorsarahgtomlinson

Or check out her books under Sarah G Tomlinson at Amazon and other book retailers.

God, all glory goes to you. Thank you for giving me dreams and a passion for writing your words, reaching your children and loving your people. I pray this book worships you and brings comfort to your daughters.

A big thank you to everyone who has supported my writing and not only encouraged, but also journeyed with me. Thank you for reading my heart notes and sharing your own personal stories. You have blessed me more than you will ever know.

A big hug for my editor Kim Burger who is not only there to make my words shine, but also my friend and overseas sister. I treasure you more than you will ever know. I love you.

To my beautiful friend Lauren Lamont, you are my rock. Thank you for always supporting me and reminding me that I am never alone on this journey. And I want to remind you that you are never alone either. As you always say, "God's got this!"

And to my husband and three boys—you are my life. The way you all support what I do and cheer me on, keeps me going. God blessed me beyond my wildest dreams. I never thought I would receive the gifts I have. But when I look at you all, I would want nothing else. You all are my purpose.

Scriptures taken from the Holy Bible, New International Version®, NIV®. Copyright © 1973, 1978, 1984, 2011 by Biblica, Inc.™ Used by permission of Zondervan. All rights reserved worldwide. www.zondervan.com The "NIV" and "New International Version" are trademarks registered in the United States Patent and Trademark Office by Biblica, Inc.™

Bonus Gifts.

As a special bonus for purchasing this book and supporting me, I would love to bless you with a pretty digital gift pack!

Simply head to
www.littlesparrowloved.com/messyandlovedgift

Then all you need to do is type in the code below to gain access.

CODE

MESSYLOVEDGIFT

Printed in Great Britain
by Amazon